12 SUPER-STRONG ANIMALS
YOU NEED TO KNOW

by Tammy Gagne

12 STORY LIBRARY

www.12StoryLibrary.com

12-Story Library is an imprint of Peterson Publishing Company and Press Room Editions.

Produced for 12-Story Library by Red Line Editorial

Photographs ©: mason01/iStockphoto, cover, 1; John Michael Evan Potter/Shutterstock Images, 4; apiguide/Shutterstock Images, 5; Elliot Hurwitt/iStockphoto, 6; Guenter Guni/ iStockphoto, 7; Holly Kuchera/iStockphoto, 8; John Alves/iStockphoto, 9; Patrick K. Campbell/Shutterstock Images, 10; David Persson/Shutterstock Images, 11; Lauren Pretorius/iStockphoto, 12; Moments_by_Mullineux/iStockphoto, 13, 28; Kyslynskyy/ iStockphoto, 14; Paula Connelly/iStockphoto, 15; michaklootwijk/iStockphoto, 16; Stephen Meese/Shutterstock Images, 17; Andyworks/iStockphoto, 18; Vladimir Melnik/Shutterstock Images, 19; Sutthaburawonk/iStockphoto, 20; wonderisland/Shutterstock Images, 21; hphimagelibrary/iStockphoto, 22, 29; anopdesignstock/iStockphoto, 23; John Carnemolla/ iStockphoto, 24; René Lorenz/iStockphoto, 25; Global_Pics/iStockphoto, 26; eROMAZe/ iStockphoto, 27

ISBN
978-1-63235-142-5 (hardcover)
978-1-63235-184-5 (paperback)
978-1-62143-236-4 (hosted ebook)

Library of Congress Control Number: 2015934280

Printed in the United States of America
Mankato, MN
June, 2015

Go beyond the book. Get free, up-to-date content on this topic at 12StoryLibrary.com.

TABLE OF CONTENTS

AFRICAN CROWNED EAGLES GRASP THEIR PREY

The African crowned eagle is the most powerful eagle species in the world. It weighs between 10 and 12 pounds (4.5 to 5.4 kg), but hunts a variety of larger animals. In addition to other birds, the African crowned eagle can kill adult mongooses and porcupines.

African crowned eagles live up to 14 years. These strong birds live in forests, rain forests, and savannas in Africa. The African crowned eagle's long tail and short wings help it fly in between the trees in search of prey.

African crowned eagles have thick legs. They use these super-strong limbs for attacking their prey. Long, sharp talons help African crowned eagles grab other animals. As the eagles catch their prey, the talons can break the animal's spine. This move often kills the prey instantly.

Crowned eagles have long crest feathers with white tips on their heads.

8

Size, in feet (2.4 m), of some African crowned eagle nests.

- African crowned eagles live in the forests of central and southeastern Africa.
- African crowned eagles nest in trees as high as 40 to 150 feet (12 to 46 m) from the ground.
- One of the strongest parts of the eagle's body is its wings. Long before they can fly, young birds flap their wings over and over to build their flight muscles.
- Female African crowned eagles are usually larger than the males.

Some of the eagle's prey is more than four times its size. African crowned eagles often prey on samango and vervet monkeys. If the prey outweighs the eagle, it will swoop to the ground to eat where the animal is. But the eagle can carry a 17-pound (7.7-kg) vervet monkey back to its nest.

The eagle's talons allow it to take down its prey without a fight.

GORILLAS HAVE LARGE ARM MUSCLES

The gorilla is the largest ape in the world. Standing six feet (1.8 m) tall, males can weigh as much as 485 pounds (220 kg). Females are a bit smaller. They can stand up to five feet (1.5 m) tall and weigh as much as 200 pounds (91 kg). Along with their size, gorillas have incredible strength. This powerful species can lift up to 10 times its own weight—or an object as heavy as a car.

A gorilla's arms are both longer and stronger than its legs. This is because its larger muscles are located in the arms. These animals spend a lot of time bending down

Male silverback gorillas use their strength to protect their families from predators.

while gathering plants to eat. Young gorillas build their arm muscles through constant play. They love to climb trees and chase one another by swinging on the branches.

Gorillas also use their strength for defending themselves. Living in groups called troops, these large apes are highly protective of their family members. A gorilla will charge at any animal that poses a danger to its troop.

Gorillas are found in the mountains and forests of Africa. These strong animals can live up to 50 years in the wild. They spend their days searching for food such as bamboo, stems, and fruits.

50
Number of years a gorilla can live.

- Gorillas are approximately 10 times stronger than a full-grown man.
- Similar to a human, a gorilla has fingerprints that are different from all other gorillas.
- Gorillas are highly intelligent. People have even taught some gorillas how to communicate using sign language.
- The word *gorilla* comes from a Greek word meaning "a tribe of hairy women."

Between six and twelve gorillas live together in a troop.

GRAY WOLVES PACK POWERFUL BITE

Gray wolves look similar to domestic dogs. But they are wild animals that can take care of themselves. Wolves live together in packs. They work together when hunting. By doing so, they can take down animals as large as deer, elk, and even moose.

Gray wolf packs live in many different habitats including forests and grasslands across North America. The average wolf is three to five feet (0.91 to 1.5 m) long. Males can weigh up to 145 pounds (66 kg), while females are slightly smaller. Gray wolves in the wild can live 13 years or longer.

The wolf's jaw strength is one of its most powerful traits. It takes one of these powerful predators just six to eight bites to crush a moose's leg bone. The wolf then eats the marrow hidden within the bone.

A gray wolf's coat helps keep it warm in colder climates.

The gray wolf's strong legs make it a fast runner.

A gray wolf's body is also strong. Its long legs have powerful muscles. Just as important, the gray wolf can keep running for long periods of time. They usually outlast their prey when chasing after it.

6

Average number of wolves in a pack.

- A gray wolf's sense of smell is 100 times more powerful than a human's.
- An adult gray wolf has a total of 42 teeth.
- A gray wolf can run up to 38 miles per hour (56 km/h) in short bursts.
- A gray wolf can eat as much as 22.5 pounds (10 kg) of meat at one time. The animal does this because it may go days or weeks between meals.

A CRUSHING BITE

Wolves have several different types of teeth. They use fangs for gripping and cutting into prey. The incisors help the gray wolf rip small pieces of meat from the carcass. They also have scissor-like teeth that act as knives. These teeth remove meat from the bones. It is the molars, though, that the wolf uses for crushing and grinding bones.

GREEN ANACONDAS SQUEEZE THE COMPETITION

The largest snake in the world is also the strongest. The powerful green anaconda does not kill with its bite. Instead, it kills prey by wrapping itself around the animal and squeezing. The squeezing kills the animal. The snake then swallows the prey whole. Snakes that do this are called constrictors.

Green anacondas are big in every way. First, they are long. Some measure more than 29 feet (8.8 m). Second, they are heavy. This species can weigh more than 550 pounds (249 kg). Third—and perhaps most striking—is the thickness of their bodies. Some green anacondas are

Green anacondas use their size and strength to overpower large animals.

more than 12 inches (30 cm) around.

These snakes can move faster in the water than they can on land.

Green anacondas can eat deer, wild pigs, and sometimes even jaguars. The anaconda is one of the few animals that kill jaguars. Jaguars bite and scratch when attacked by an anaconda. The big cats tire quickly, though. By the time the snake starts squeezing, the jaguar does not have enough strength left to keep up the fight. In longer battles, the anaconda usually comes out on top.

Green anacondas live in northern South America. They move through the swamps and marshes of the South American rain forests.

10

Average number of years a green anaconda lives.

- Green anacondas live in the swamps and streams of South America.
- They sometimes drag their prey under water to drown it.
- Anacondas are not venomous. Their jaws can still deliver a powerful bite, however.
- Green anacondas wait for prey to come to them. As soon as it is close enough, they grab it.

THINK ABOUT IT

In what kind of situation do you think a jaguar would win a fight against a green anaconda? What traits do you think each animal has that would help it get the upper hand?

HONEY BADGERS ARE STRONG AND FEARLESS

The honey badger does not look strong. Looks can be deceiving, though. Even animals much larger than the honey badger try to stay away from this fierce predator. The species has been known to kill and eat wildebeest, waterbuck, and even large pythons. Refusing to give up, the honey badger will fight to the death. In most cases the other animal gets tired, falling victim to the honey badger's constant bites.

The honey badger has thick skin. This tough covering helps protect it from the bites and stings of some dangerous creatures. Some honey badgers have lived despite being bitten by scorpions or venomous snakes.

The honey badger has a thick white stripe that runs down its back. The marking makes the animal look similar to a skunk. And that is not the only thing honey badgers share with this smelly species. Like skunks, honey badgers have a special gland that releases a stinky liquid when the animal feels threatened.

Honey badgers can live up to 26 years in captivity. It is unclear how long they live in the wild. In the wild, honey badgers live in forests and deserts in Africa and the Middle East. These small animals climb trees in search of honey.

A honey badger uses its strong teeth to kill its prey.

2

Age a honey badger is ready to leave its mother and venture out on its own.

- As its name suggests, honey badgers' favorite food is honey.
- Honey badgers will do almost anything to get to honey—even suffer numerous bee stings.
- Honey badgers weigh around 15 pounds (6.8 kg).
- While all honey badgers are vicious to other animals, females are caring and gentle mothers.

THINK ABOUT IT

One might say that the strongest thing about the honey badger is its attitude. Based on what you have read about the animal here, would you agree with this statement? Find sentences that support your answer.

Honey badgers look and act similar in some ways to skunks.

JAGUARS' POWERFUL JAWS CRUSH PREY

Jaguars are among the world's strongest animals. These large South American cats sit quietly in high spots waiting for prey. Once an animal comes near, the sneaky jaguar pounces on it from above.

Other big cats kill their prey by biting its neck. But the super-strong jaguar can crush another animal's skull with a single bite. The jaguar's jaws apply 2,000 pounds (907 kg) of bite pressure. This enormous force kills the prey instantly.

But the jaguar does not stop there. Once its prey is dead, the jaguar often drags its food up a tree before eating it. It does not want to have to fight another predator for the reward. Some of the animal carcasses are impressively large. The jaguar's strength enables it to kill and drag animals as big as 660 pounds (300 kg).

Jaguars live to be up to 15 years old. These big cats grow to be six feet (1.8 m) long, not including their tail.

Jaguars use their powerful muscles for climbing steep slopes and trees.

15,000

Number of jaguars living in the wild today.

- Weighing from 100 to 250 pounds (45 to 113 kg), the jaguar is the largest cat in South America.
- The jaguar got its name from the American Indian word *yaguar*. It means "he who kills with one leap."
- The spots of dark-colored jaguars blend into their coats. Many people mistakenly think these cats have no spots at all.
- Jaguars are top predators where they live. They can kill nearly any other animal in the area.

Young jaguars learn to hunt for fish, turtles, and deer from their mothers. These young will grow to be up to 250 pounds (113 kg) as adults.

CRACKING SHELLS

Jaguars eat turtles and tortoises. Some jaguars simply bite off the edge of the turtle shell. Then they pull the prey out before eating it. But the jaguar can actually bite right through the shell when necessary. Its powerful jaws can even crack the shells of large tortoises. These land animals are much bigger than turtles found in rivers and streams.

LEAFCUTTER ANTS CARRY THEIR FOOD

Even small animals can be strong. The leafcutter ant weighs just 0.0003 ounces (0.01 g). This is about the same size as a grain of rice. But this tiny insect can carry between three and six times its own weight.

Like other ants, members of this species search for food. They load themselves with as much plant material as they can carry. Because leafcutter ants are so strong, they can make a huge dent in crops. While most ants prefer seeds, they will also eat grains, grasses, and leaves. Farmers rank them as one of their worst pests for this reason.

The tiny pieces of leaves that leafcutter ants carry may not seem like much at first. But the feat is much like a human adult carrying 660 pounds (300 kg). Even with all of this weight, the leafcutter ant moves fast.

Leafcutter ants take as much food as possible back to their nest.

A comparable speed would be a human adult running a four-minute mile. Imagine a runner keeping up this speed while carrying four other people!

A POWERFUL CRUNCH

It is not just the leafcutter ant's body that is fast and strong. This ant's powerful jaws also make it one of the most amazing animals on the planet. A leafcutter ant can move its jaws up and down 1,000 times per second to bite pieces off leaves. This action is where the ant gets its name.

20

Amount, in tons (18 metric tons), of soil that a leafcutter ant moves in its lifetime.

- Leafcutter ants eat approximately 20 percent of the entire plant growth in South America each year.
- Leafcutter ants improve soil quality where they search for food. They add air to the soil and remove waste from it.
- Leafcutter ant colonies can contain up to 5 million members.
- American Indians once used the jaws of leafcutter ants as stitches to hold wounds closed.

Leafcutter ants work together to build their colony.

OXEN ARE HARD WORKERS

There is a reason that people use the phrase "as strong as an ox." Before the invention of the tractor, oxen were among a farmer's most valued resources. By pulling plows, these heavy-duty animals made it possible for farmers to grow bigger crops with much less work in the 1800s.

Even today, some farmers prefer using oxen to big machinery. Farmers who still use oxen usually have less than 50 acres (20 hectares) of crops. These strong animals can weigh between 1,500 and 3,000 pounds (680 and 1,361 kg). This massive size helps them pull plows, logs, or other materials even heavier than their own weight.

Oxen perform their work just as well as modern machinery. Where they lose the contest is the amount of time they take. It takes a pair of oxen a whole day to plow one acre (0.4 hectare) of land.

Oxen are much cheaper for farmers than buying new machinery.

Many small farms use oxen.

300 million

Number of oxen still being used by farmers worldwide today.

- A trained steer must be at least five years old to be called an ox.
- Not all steers trained actually become oxen. Some do not learn the commands well enough to perform the work needed.
- Oxen work in pairs and can live between 15 and 20 years.

STEERS WITH JOBS

The word *ox* is not the name of a species. Dairy or beef cattle are called oxen when they are trained for pulling heavy items. One might say that oxen are cattle with jobs. The average ox learns five basic commands: go forward, turn right, turn left, back up, and stop.

RHINOCEROS BEETLES USE THEIR HORNS

Imagine a person lifting nine elephants. It is hard to picture! Of course, this task is impossible for a person. A rhinoceros beetle, on the other hand, can lift items 850 times its own weight. That is about the same as a human holding up those nine elephants.

The rhinoceros beetle is named for the horn on the head of male members of the species. It makes the beetle look a bit like a rhinoceros. The horns help the beetles dig into the earth. This ability comes in handy for avoiding predators, such as birds, skunks, and snakes.

Some people call this insect the Hercules beetle.

6

Length, in inches (15 cm), a rhinoceros beetle can grow.

- Rhinoceros beetles make a hissing noise when disturbed. They produce the sound by rubbing their abdomens against their wing covers.
- They are found on every continent in the world except Antarctica.
- Rhinoceros beetles can live up to two years.
- Female rhinoceros beetles will lay approximately 50 eggs at a time.

Males will fight each other during mating season.

Male rhinoceros beetles also use their horns for fighting one another over females. This species does not use its horn for chasing after prey, however. They eat fruit, nectar, and plant matter—not other insects.

RHINOCEROSES GAIN STRENGTH FROM THEIR SIZE

The rhinoceros is one of the largest animals on the planet. Two species of rhinos exist today in Africa. A black rhino can weigh as much as 3,080 pounds (1,397 kg). A white rhinoceros can be even bigger—up to 7,920 pounds (3,590 kg). That is heavier than most cars.

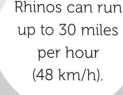

Rhinos can run up to 30 miles per hour (48 km/h).

A rhino's size gives these animals a fair amount of strength. Add its powerful horns, and it is a creature few other animals want to go up

IS THAT AN ENEMY?

Some black rhinos will charge at trees or termite mounds. One reason for this odd behavior may be the rhino's poor eyesight. Most rhinos will not notice a person standing 100 feet (30 m) away unless the person moves. The animal's hearing and sense of smell are excellent, however.

against in a fight. While each rhino has two horns, it is the front horn that it uses for fighting. Rhinos eat plants, not meat. They will defend themselves from predators such as lions, though. During a fight a rhinoceros will use its front horn to spear the other animal.

A black rhinoceros usually gets along with members of its own species. But it will charge at other animals if it senses an attack. Male and female rhinos use their horns to fight off attackers and protect their offspring.

Rhinos live up to 40 years in the wild.

5

Length, in feet (1.5 m), a white rhino's front horn can grow.

- A young rhinoceros is not able to live on its own until it is around three years old.
- White rhinos are less aggressive than black rhinos.
- Black rhinos are actually gray in color.
- Both black and white rhinos are often killed for their horns. Some people in Asia use the horns to make certain medicines.

SALTWATER CROCODILES HOLD ON TO THEIR PREY

The largest crocodile species is also the strongest. A saltwater crocodile can grow as long as 23 feet (7 m) and weigh up to 2,200 pounds (1,000 kg). Even the smallest saltwater crocs are four times bigger than an average-sized human.

The crocodile's body is strong. Its tail can deliver a powerful thrashing. But it is the saltwater croc's jaws that make it one of the strongest animals. Once this species bites down, it is nearly impossible for anyone or anything to open its jaw.

The saltwater croc is a top predator in and near the Pacific Ocean. Salties, as they are called, use their mighty jaws for hunting a wide variety of prey. They eat monkeys, sharks, and even water buffalo.

Saltwater crocodiles blend in with their habitats.

Once the croc bites down, its prey is unlikely to get away. The muscles that open a croc's mouth are not nearly as strong as the ones that close them, however. A rubber band is strong enough to keep a croc's mouth shut.

300,000
Number of saltwater crocodiles living today.

- Saltwater crocodiles can live to be 70 years old.
- Although they are called saltwater crocodiles, they can also live in freshwater.
- The crocodile's powerful tail makes it a strong swimmer.

THINK ABOUT IT

Based on the information you have read above, which type of prey do you think has the best chance against a saltwater crocodile? Give evidence to support your answer.

TIGERS SWIPE WITH STRONG PAWS

The first thing you may notice about a tiger is its size. These large cats can weigh up to 500 pounds (230 kg). They use this size and the power that comes with it for hunting animals such as deer and wild boar. Tigers are patient predators, waiting until just the right moment to strike.

The prey does not have to be close, however. A tiger's strong legs help the animal jump more than 30 feet (9.1 m) in a single leap. It then uses its front legs to force the prey to the ground. Few animals escape this mighty hunter.

A tiger may use its paws to kill its

A tiger's teeth come in handy when it shreds its prey apart.

SPLISH, SPLASH!

House cats may not like the water. But tigers love it. These large cats are excellent swimmers. Being in the water does not stop tigers from hunting either. Some tigers even kill prey while swimming.

Once the prey is close enough, the tiger pounces.

10

Number of days a tiger often goes without eating.

- Most tigers wait for prey to come to them. But they can still run fast—up to 50 miles per hour (80 km/h).
- A tiger's teeth can measure up to three inches (7.6 cm) in length.
- Its claws can grow up to five inches (13 cm) long.
- Three tiger species have already become extinct. No more Bali, Caspian, or Javan tigers are left in the world.

prey. It can snap the spinal cord of smaller animals with a single swipe from its front paw. This large cat also has strong jaws. It may use them to grab and cut the throat of larger prey. This action also kills the animal quickly.

FACT SHEET

- Many super-strong animals, like saltwater crocodiles, use their strength for catching and killing prey. Still other species, like the rhinoceros beetle, rely on their strength for fighting over possible mates.

- Animals can be strong in many different ways. Some, like the jaguar, are strong on land. Others, like the anaconda, are strong in water as well. Likewise, some animals deliver powerful bites while others use their bodies to overpower prey.

- Strength can also be measured differently. A leafcutter ant cannot lift the same amount of weight as an ox can pull. But when you consider its size, the ant is actually the stronger animal.

- Even the strongest animals may not always win a fight against another animal. Strength only matters when one animal can catch another. If a strong animal goes up against a faster animal, the faster one often has the advantage of escape.

- Strength takes time to develop. Jaguars may be top predators. But their young are at risk of being killed by larger animals. When a mother jaguar is not there to defend them, her young cubs cannot win a fight against a hungry anaconda.

GLOSSARY

carcass
The body of a dead animal.

constrictor
A snake that kills its prey by wrapping its body around it and crushing it.

domestic
Kept as a farm animal or pet.

extinct
No longer existing.

incisor
A front tooth used for cutting.

marrow
A soft, yellowish tissue within the bone that is rich in nutrients.

nectar
A sweet liquid made by plants.

predator
An animal that preys on others for food.

prey
An animal that is hunted or killed by another for food.

talon
A claw of an animal, especially that of a large bird.

venomous
Capable of putting poison into another animal's body.

FOR MORE INFORMATION

Books

Animal Encyclopedia: 2,500 Animals with Photos, Maps, and More!
    Washington, DC: National Geographic, 2012.

Ipcizade, Catherine. *The Strongest Animals*. Mankato, MN: Capstone Press,
    2011.

Murray, Julie. *Strongest Animals*. Minneapolis: ABDO Publishing, 2010.

Websites

African Wildlife Foundation: Rhinoceros
www.awf.org/wildlife-conservation/rhinoceros

National Wildlife Federation: Rhinoceros Beetle
www.nwf.org/wildlife/wildlife-library/invertebrates/rhinoceros-beetles.aspx

World Wildlife Foundation: Tiger
www.worldwildlife.org/species/tiger

INDEX

About the Author

Tammy Gagne has written more than 100 books for both adults and children. She resides in northern New England with her husband and son. One of her favorite pastimes is visiting schools to talk to children about the writing process.

READ MORE FROM 12-STORY LIBRARY

Every 12-Story Library book is available in many formats, including Amazon Kindle and Apple iBooks. For more information, visit your device's store or 12StoryLibrary.com.